INSIGHTS
Christmas

What the Bible Tells Us about the
Christmas Story

WILLIAM BARCLAY

SAINT ANDREW PRESS
Edinburgh

First published in 2008 by
SAINT ANDREW PRESS
121 George Street
Edinburgh EH2 4YN

ISBN 978 0 7152 0858 8

British Library Cataloguing in Publication Data
A catalogue record for this book is available from the British Library

It is the Publisher's policy to only use papers that are natural and
recyclable and that have been manufactured from timber grown in
renewable, properly managed forests. All of the manufacturing
processes of the papers are expected to conform to the environmental
regulations of the country of origin.

Typeset by Waverley Typesetters, Fakenham
Printed and bound by Bell & Bain Ltd, Glasgow

Contents

Foreword by
The Right Revd Nick Baines

It is the most dramatic night of the year – one that confronts a waiting humanity with the mystery of the Creator becoming subject to the creation – God becoming vulnerable to life and death in a mortal and messy world. Or is it?

Not a December goes by without my being torn by a terrible internal tension: do I celebrate the festival regardless of the serious side of the Nativity events or do I rebel against the nonsense that has become Christmas? It isn't just the tinsel and shopping-fest that gets to me, but also how the churches often seem to collude in reducing the Christmas story to something resembling a sentimentalised Victorian family scene complete with fluffy animals and beautiful white children frolicking carelessly in the snow.

The problem is not hard to understand. Generations of children have learned that Jesus was born on a 'silent night'. Not only was nothing happening out there, but, apparently, 'no crying he made'. Then, to make matters worse, the same children are spiritually blackmailed into becoming 'mild, obedient, good as he'. These lyrics lead us into the realm of fantasy (did this child live on the same planet as the rest of us?) and are then compounded by school plays that dream up cattle, donkeys and sheep – and these days even introduce lobsters and any other creature that gives every child a role in the fiction being acted out.

They say that children now grow up and throw out the benign bearded elderly God along with Father Christmas, eliding both into a single imaginary figure and not seeing any further connection with the real world we experience every day. Out go the Tooth Fairy, Jesus of Nazareth and Santa's little elves. And we wonder why it is so difficult to help adults move beyond this misconception and find again the power of the Christmas story.

Part of the reason for this is simply that we have forgotten how to wait. In an 'instant' culture, we expect to have our needs and desires met immediately. But the Christmas story can only be understood and lived in by those who have learned how to wait for God. God's people had been looking and longing for the return of their Lord for four hundred years during which he seemed to be silent. When God finally came to his people he did so in an absurdly slow way. Why didn't he come with fanfares and blazing guns? Why come through a womb after a nine-month pregnancy with all its inherent dangers and then emerge as a vulnerable baby into an occupied country dominated by one of the most efficiently ruthless empires in history? Well, that is how God chose to do it and that is why the Christmas story begins with a long silence, a glimpse of the generations that had gone before and the ending of the wait – not with a bang, but the whimper of a baby in a borrowed manger. Unless, of course, he was the only baby in history never to have cried.

This is a very strange God for a world which understands power and might in terms of strength and domination. He almost seems ridiculous. Yet, those who waited and looked for him would remember how the oppressors had always mocked God's people for trusting in their God while the evidence of their circumstances suggested he was simply not there. 'How can we sing the Lord's song in a strange land' was not a line from a pop song, but a cry wrenched from the guts of a people who had been humiliated by a pagan empire and challenged to drop their apparently absurd faith. But the Bible tells us that God's people have to learn to wait for him – that his apparent silence is not to be confused with his eternal absence.

In one sense, we should not be surprised by God coming among us in such a small way. After all, the adult Jesus seemed to be at pains to depict the 'kingdom' of God (or *Godzone* as Mike Riddell termed it) as something small. A mustard seed is tiny and can be trampled into the ground by careless feet; but it can grow into a tree whose branches are convenient for hosting the nests of birds who have not been specifically invited to live there.

This leads us on to note that the gospel narratives of the public ministry of Jesus pose tough questions to a world that likes to choose its friends according to taste and status. Jesus eventually got himself crucified by the religious professionals after having surrounded himself with a ragbag of not-very-hopeful disciples for several years. Even a cursory read through the gospels indicates that the people who welcomed Jesus and responded to him were those who had been discarded by the kosher establishment as being in various ways 'unclean' or unfitting.

This being the case, then, perhaps it is not surprising that the two gospels that describe the events of the first Christmas give star-billing to the most unlikely people. Shepherds are rough, working men who are of low status; Magi are pagan astrologers from foreign parts; even the genealogies include several dodgy women. In other words, neither would be expected to be introduced to the young Jesus ahead of priests, religious keenies and other worthy and deserving righteous people.

This seems to be suggesting that right from the outset of the gospel narratives, we are supposed to recognise the shocking fact that God (in Christ) is one of us, is on our side, is with us (Immanuel) and is for us. The ordinary person who meets Jesus with no self-righteousness, but only a recognition of need, finds here a place of welcome and a relationship that turns upside-down the assumptions of the world in which we live. God believes in us enough to come among us and share our life. And never can we point the finger to God and accuse him of remaining in a safe place, away from the realities of the world in which we live.

When I conducted my son's wedding a few days after Christmas 2007 I noted that many people had brought presents and cards wrapped in paper bearing fluffy pink love hearts. Though welcome, the pink heart is not an adequate icon of love; it is merely romantic and sentimental. I went on to offer another icon of love – one that has a man on a cross, arms outstretched in welcome to the world, allowing us to throw at him what we will and refusing to throw it back at us. This icon of genuine love bears the pain and faces the realities of the world in which we live and move and have our being.

This is why Christmas is meaningless without Easter and Easter is pointless without Christmas. Easter without Christmas easily leads to an abstract and disembodied 'salvation' from sin, whereas Christmas without Easter leaves us with a nice idea (*logos*) that quickly ran out of steam.

So, Christmas is about God coming into the world with which we are familiar: ambiguous, challenging, beautiful, surprising, glorious and painful. He comes in the small and lets himself be subject to it. He takes his time and will not be rushed. He challenges our expectations and opens our eyes and minds to a different way of seeing and thinking and living. And he makes me want to re-write yet another favourite Christmas carol so that we sing to a waiting world: 'O come, all ye faithless'. Christmas is a quiet yet reckless invitation to a cynical world to recognise God behaving oddly and coming among us as one of us – thus offering to the most unlikely people a hope that will never disappoint. After all, the crucifixion mentioned earlier was not to be the end of the story.

William Barclay writes with such an intelligent clarity and generosity that you can almost see and hear and smell the place in which Christmas slid into the world. Much has been written on the so-called 'birth narratives', but Barclay manages to encapsulate in short passages the essence of the events and compel us to want to know what happened next. In the introductory commentaries to the Gospels of Matthew and Luke he makes us aware of details that bring the narrative alive and distance it from the tinsel and fantasy of Xmas.

In this short book, William Barclay takes us into the heart of the Christmas story, painting the detail of the text of the opening chapters of the two Gospels onto the larger canvas of God's incarnation in Jesus. This book will take us into Christmas, but, like a good television serial, it will leave us wanting to know what happened next and why.

Nick Baines

Publisher's Introduction

We all know the story of the wise men. They visited Herod and their news troubled him. They followed a star and found the baby Jesus and offered gifts of gold, frankincense and myrrh.

That's all in the Bible.

Some people say that the wise men were kings and that there were three of them. Some people can even name them – Casper, Melchior and Balthaser.

But that's not in the Bible.

Insights: Christmas explains what the Bible really says, and *why*.

Because of his gift for clear explanation and insight, author William Barclay has millions of fans across the globe. He believed that it makes all the difference *who* said something, *when* they said it, *how* they said it, *where* they said it and *to whom* it was said. So he made his own modern text of the New Testament by translating from the original Greek and then commented on the stories by considering, afresh, the particular circumstances of each writer. He made clear what was meant, what was possibly meant and, as in the example of the naming of the three wise men, what may have inspired the legends.

Each book in the *Insights* series takes a particular theme and allows the reader to engage with the New Testament, bringing the people and the times to life. For example, this book shows that, in the Christmas story we all know so well, the wise men appear only in Matthew's Gospel and the shepherds in Luke's. *Insights* makes no assumptions about our knowledge, but enables us to understand the Bible in new ways by starting with something familiar and then finding some surprising twists in the tale.

Introduction to Matthew

The gospel of the Jews

First and foremost, Matthew is *the gospel which was written for the Jews*. It was written by a Jew in order to convince Jews.

One of the great objects of Matthew is to demonstrate that all the prophecies of the Old Testament are fulfilled in Jesus, and that, therefore, he must be the Messiah. It has one phrase which runs through it like an ever-recurring theme: 'This was to fulfil what the Lord had spoken by the prophet.' That phrase occurs in the gospel as often as sixteen times. Jesus' birth and Jesus' name are the fulfilment of prophecy (1:21–3); so are the flight to Egypt (2:14–15); the slaughter of the children (2:16–18); Joseph's settlement in Nazareth and Jesus' upbringing there (2:23); Jesus' use of parables (3:34–5); the triumphal entry (21:3–5); the betrayal for thirty pieces of silver (27:9); and the casting of lots for Jesus' garments as he hung on the cross (27:35). It is Matthew's primary and deliberate purpose to show how the Old Testament prophecies received their fulfilment in Jesus; how every detail of Jesus' life was foreshadowed in the prophets; and thus to compel the Jews to admit that Jesus was the Messiah.

The main interest of Matthew is in the Jews. Their conversion is especially near and dear to the heart of its writer. When the Syro-Phoenician woman seeks his help, Jesus' first answer is: 'I was sent only to the lost sheep of the house of Israel' (15:24). When Jesus sends out the Twelve on the task of evangelization, his instruction is: 'Go nowhere among the Gentiles, and enter no town of the Samaritans, but go rather to the lost sheep of the house of Israel' (10:5–6). Yet it is not to be thought that this gospel by any means excludes the Gentiles. Many are to come from the east and the west to sit down in the kingdom of God (8:11). The gospel is to be preached to the whole world (24:14). And it is Matthew which gives us the marching orders of the Church: 'Go therefore and make disciples of all nations' (28:19). It is clear that Matthew's first interest is in the Jews, but that it foresees the day when all nations will be gathered in.

The teaching gospel

The apostle Matthew was responsible for the first collection and the first handbook of the teaching of Jesus. Matthew was the great systematizer. It was his habit to gather together in one place all that he knew about the teaching of Jesus on any given subject. The result is that in Matthew we find five great blocks in which the teaching of Jesus is collected and systematized. All these sections have to do with the kingdom of God. They are as follows:

(a) The Sermon on the Mount, or the law of the kingdom (5–7).

(b) The duties of the leaders of the kingdom (10).

(c) The parables of the kingdom (13).

(d) Greatness and forgiveness in the kingdom (18).

(e) The coming of the King (24–5).

Matthew does more than collect and systematize. It must be remembered that Matthew was writing in an age when printing had not been invented, when books were few and far between because they had to be handwritten. In an age like that, comparatively few people could possess a book; and, therefore, if they wished to know and to use the teaching and the story of Jesus, they had to carry them in their memories.

Matthew therefore always arranges things in a way that is easy for the reader to memorize. He arranges things in threes and sevens. There are three messages to Joseph; three denials of Peter; three questions of Pilate; seven parables of the kingdom in chapter 13; and seven woes to the scribes and Pharisees in chapter 23.

The genealogy of Jesus with which the gospel begins is a good example of this. The genealogy is to prove that Jesus is the Son of David. In Hebrew there are no figures; when figures are necessary, the letters of the alphabet stand for the figures. In Hebrew there are no written vowels. The Hebrew letters for David are DWD; if these letters are taken as figures and not as letters, they add up to fourteen; and the genealogy consists of three groups of names, and in each group there are fourteen names. Matthew does everything possible to arrange the teaching of Jesus in such a way that people will be able to assimilate and to remember it.

Matthew has one final characteristic. Matthew's *dominating idea is that of Jesus as King.* He writes to demonstrate the royalty of Jesus.

Right at the beginning, the genealogy is to prove that Jesus is the Son of David (1:1–17). The title, Son of David, is used more often in Matthew than in any other gospel (15:22, 21:9, 21:15). The wise men come looking for him who is King of the

Jews (2:2). The triumphal entry is a deliberately dramatized claim to be King (21:1–11). Before Pilate, Jesus deliberately accepts the name of King (27:11). Even on the cross, the title of King is affixed, even if it is in mockery, over his head (27:37). In the Sermon on the Mount, Matthew shows us Jesus quoting the law and five times abrogating it with a regal: 'But I say to you ...' (5:22, 28, 34, 39, 44). The final claim of Jesus is: 'All authority ... has been given to me' (28:18).

Matthew's picture of Jesus is of the man born to be King. Jesus walks through his pages as if in the purple and gold of royalty.

Matthew

The lineage of the king

IT might seem to a modern reader that Matthew chose an extraordinary way in which to begin his gospel; and it might seem daunting to present right at the beginning a long list of names to wade through. But to a Jew this was the most natural, and the most interesting, and indeed the most essential way to begin the story of any man's life.

Matthew 1:1–17

This is the record of the lineage of Jesus Christ, the Son of David, the son of Abraham.

Abraham begat Isaac, and Isaac begat Jacob. Jacob begat Judah and his brothers. Judah begat Phares and Zara, whose mother was Thamar. Phares begat Esrom. Esrom begat Aram. Aram begat Aminadab. Aminadab begat Naasson. Naasson begat Salmon. Salmon begat Booz, whose mother was Rachab. Booz begat Obed, whose mother was Ruth. Obed begat Jesse. Jesse begat David, the king.

David begat Solomon, whose mother was Uriah's wife. Solomon begat Roboam. Roboam begat Abia. Abia begat Asaph. Asaph begat Josaphat. Josaphat begat Joram. Joram begat Ozias. Ozias begat Joatham. Joatham begat Achaz.

Achaz begat Ezekias. Ezekias begat Manasses. Manasses begat Amos. Amos begat Josias. Josias begat Jechonias, and his brothers, in the days when the exile to Babylon took place.

After the exile to Babylon Jechonias begat Salathiel. Salathiel begat Zorobabel. Zorobabel begat Abioud. Abioud begat Eliakim. Eliakim begat Azor. Azor begat Zadok. Zadok begat Acheim. Acheim begat Elioud. Elioud begat Eleazar. Eleazar begat Matthan. Matthan begat Jacob. Jacob begat Joseph, the husband of Mary, who was the mother of Jesus, who is called Christ.

From Abraham to David there were in all fourteen generations. From David to the exile to Babylon there were also fourteen generations. From the exile to Babylon to the coming of Christ there were also fourteen generations.

The Jews were exceedingly interested in genealogies. Matthew calls this *the book of the generation* (*biblos geneseōs*) of Jesus Christ. That to the Jews was a common phrase; and it means the record of a man's lineage, with a few explanatory sentences, where such comment was necessary. In the Old Testament, we frequently find lists of the *generations* of famous men (Genesis 5:1, 10:1, 11:10, 11:27). When Josephus, the great Jewish historian, wrote his own autobiography, he began it with his own pedigree, which, he tells us, he found in the public records.

The reason for this interest in pedigrees was that the Jews set the greatest possible store on purity of lineage. If in any man there was the slightest element of foreign blood, he lost his right to be called a Jew and a member of the people of God. A priest, for instance, was bound to produce an unbroken record of his pedigree stretching back to Aaron; and, if he married, the woman he married must produce her pedigree for at least five generations back. When Ezra was reorganizing the worship of God after the people returned from exile, and was setting the priesthood to function again, the children of Habaiah, the children of Koz and the children of Barzillai were debarred from office and were labelled as polluted because 'These looked for their entries in the genealogical records, but they were not found there' (Ezra 2:62).

These genealogical records were actually kept by the Sanhedrin. Herod the Great was always despised by the pure-blooded Jews because he was half-Edomite; and we can see the importance that even Herod attached to these genealogies from the fact that he had the official registers destroyed, so that no one could prove a purer pedigree than his own. To a Jew, it would be a most impressive matter that the pedigree of Jesus could be traced back to Abraham.

It is further to be noted that this pedigree is most carefully arranged. It is arranged in three groups of fourteen people each. It is in fact what is technically known as a mnemonic, that is to say a thing so arranged that it is easy to memorize. It is always to be remembered that the gospels were written hundreds of years before there was any such thing as a printed book. Very few people would be able to own actual copies of them; and so, if they wished to possess them, they would be compelled to memorize them. This pedigree, therefore, is arranged in such a way that it is easy to memorize. It is meant to prove that Jesus was the Son of David, and is so arranged as to make it easy for people to carry it in their memories.

The three stages

Matthew 1:1–17 (*contd*)

THERE is something symbolic of the whole of human life in the way in which this pedigree is arranged. It is arranged in three sections, and the three sections are based on three great stages in Jewish history.

The first section takes the history down to David. David was the man who welded Israel into a nation and made the Jews a power in the world. The first section takes the story down to the rise of Israel's greatest king.

The second section takes the story down to the exile to Babylon. It is the section which tells of the nation's shame, tragedy and disaster.

The third section takes the story down to Jesus Christ. Jesus Christ was the person who liberated men and women from their slavery, who rescued them from their disaster, and in whom the tragedy was turned into triumph.

These three sections stand for three stages in the spiritual history of the world.

(1) *Human beings were born for greatness.* God created them in his own image (cf. Genesis 1:27). As the Revised Standard Version has it, God said: 'Let us make man in our image, after our likeness' (Genesis 1:26). Human beings were created in the image of God. God's dream for them was a dream of greatness. They were designed for fellowship with God; created that they might be nothing less than kin to God. As Cicero, the Roman thinker, saw it, 'The only difference between man and God is in point of time.' Human destiny was for greatness.

(2) *Human beings lost their greatness.* Instead of being the servants of God, they became slaves of sin. As the writer G. K. Chesterton said, 'whatever else is true of man, man is not what he was meant to be'. Men and women used their free will to defy and to disobey God, rather than to enter into friendship and fellowship with him. Left to themselves, they had frustrated the design and plan of God in his creation.

(3) *Human beings can regain their greatness.* Even then, God did not abandon men and women to themselves and to their own devices. God did not allow them to be destroyed by their own folly. The end of the story was not left to be tragedy. Into this world God sent his Son, Jesus Christ, that he might rescue men and women from the morass of sin in which they had lost themselves, and liberate them from the chains of sin with which they had bound themselves so that through him they might regain the fellowship with God which they had lost.

In his genealogy, Matthew shows us the royalty of kingship gained; the tragedy of freedom lost; the glory of liberty restored. And that, in the mercy of God, is the story of all humanity, and of every individual.

The realization of people's dreams

Matthew 1:1–17 (*contd*)

THIS passage stresses two special things about Jesus.

(1) It stresses the fact that he was the Son of David. It was, indeed, mainly to prove this that the genealogy was composed. The New Testament stresses this again and again.

Peter states it in the first recorded sermon of the Christian Church (Acts 2:29–36). Paul speaks of Jesus Christ descended from David according to the flesh (Romans 1:3). The writer of the Pastoral Epistles urges people to remember that Jesus Christ, descended from David, was raised from the dead (2 Timothy 2:8). The writer of the Revelation hears the risen Christ say: 'I am the root and the descendant of David' (Revelation 22:16).

Repeatedly, Jesus is addressed in this way in the gospel story. After the healing of the blind and dumb man, the people exclaim: 'Can this be the Son of David?' (Matthew 12:23). The woman of Tyre and Sidon, who wished for Jesus' help for her daughter, calls him 'Son of David' (Matthew 15:22). The blind men cry out to Jesus as Son of David (Matthew 20:30–1). It is as Son of David that the crowds greet Jesus when he enters Jerusalem for the last time (Matthew 21:9, 15).

There is something of great significance here. It is clear that it was the crowd, the ordinary men and women, who addressed Jesus as Son of David. And it was their dream that into this world would come a descendant of David who would lead them to the glory which they believed to be theirs by right.

That is to say, Jesus is the answer to the dreams of men and women. It is true that so often people do not see it so. They see the answer to their dreams in power, in wealth, in material plenty, and in the realization of the ambitions which they cherish. But if ever their dreams of peace and loveliness, and greatness and satisfaction, are to be realized, they can find their realization only in Jesus Christ.

Jesus Christ and the life he offers is the answer to the dreams of men and women. In the old Joseph story, there is a text which goes far beyond the story itself. When Joseph was in prison, Pharaoh's chief butler and chief baker were prisoners along with him. They had their dreams, and their dreams troubled them, and their bewildered cry is: 'We have had dreams, and there is no one to interpret them' (Genesis 40:8). Because we are human, because we are children of eternity, we are always haunted by our dreams; and the only way to their realization lies in Jesus Christ.

(2) This passage also stresses that Jesus was the fulfilment of prophecy. In him, the message of the prophets came true. We tend nowadays to make very little of prophecy. We are not really interested, for the most part, in searching for sayings in the Old Testament which are fulfilled in the New Testament. But prophecy does contain this great and eternal truth: that in this universe there is purpose and design and that God is meaning and willing certain things to happen.

In Gerald Healy's play *The Black Stranger*, there is a telling scene. The setting is in Ireland, in the terrible days of famine in the mid-nineteenth century. For want of something better to do, and for lack of some other solution, the government had set men to digging roads to no purpose and to no destination. Michael finds out about this and comes home one day, and says in poignant wonder to his father: 'They're makin' roads that lead to nowhere.'

If we believe in prophecy, that is what we can never say. History can never be a road that leads to nowhere. We may not use prophecy in the same way as our ancestors did, but at the back of the fact of prophecy lies the eternal fact that life and the world are not on the way to nowhere, but on the way to the goal of God.

Not the righteous, but sinners

Matthew 1:1–17 (*contd*)

By far the most amazing thing about this pedigree is the names of the women who appear in it.

It is not normal to find the names of women in Jewish pedigrees at all. Women had no legal rights; a woman was regarded not as a person, but as a thing. She was merely the possession of her father or of her husband, and therefore his to do with as he liked. In the regular form of morning prayer, the Jew thanked God that he had not made him a Gentile, a slave or a woman. The very existence of these names in any pedigree at all is a most surprising and extraordinary phenomenon.

But when we look at who these women were, and at what they did, the matter becomes even more amazing. Rachab, or as the Old Testament calls her, Rahab, was a harlot of Jericho (Joshua 2:1–7). Ruth was not even a Jewess; she was a Moabitess (Ruth 1:4); and does not the law itself lay it down, 'No Ammonite or Moabite shall be admitted to the assembly of the Lord. Even to the tenth generation, none of their descendants shall enter the assembly of the Lord' (Deuteronomy 23:3)? Ruth belonged to an alien and a hated people. Tamar was a deliberate seducer and an adulteress (Genesis 38). Bathsheba, the mother of Solomon, was the woman whom David seduced from Uriah, her husband, with an unforgivable cruelty (2 Samuel 11 and 12). If Matthew had ransacked the pages of the Old Testament for improbable candidates, he could not have discovered four more incredible ancestors for Jesus Christ. But, surely, there is something very lovely in this. Here, at the very beginning, Matthew shows us in symbol the essence of the gospel of God in Jesus Christ, for here he shows us the barriers going down.

(1) *The barrier between Jew and Gentile is down.* Rahab, the woman of Jericho, and Ruth, the woman of Moab, find their place within the pedigree of Jesus Christ. Already the great truth is there that in Christ there is neither Jew nor Greek. Here, at the very beginning, there is the universalism of the gospel and of the love of God.

(2) *The barriers between male and female are down.* In no ordinary pedigree would the name of any woman be found; but such names are found in Jesus' pedigree. The old contempt is gone; and men and women stand equally dear to God, and equally important to his purposes.

(3) *The barrier between saint and sinner is down.* Somehow God can use for his purposes, and fit into his scheme of things, those who have sinned greatly. 'I have come', said Jesus, 'to call not the righteous, but sinners' (Matthew 9:13).

Here at the very beginning of the gospel, we are given a hint of the all-embracing width of the love of God. God can find his servants among those from whom the respectable orthodox would shrink away in horror.

The Saviour's entry into the world

Matthew 1:18–25

The birth of Jesus Christ happened in this way. Mary, his mother, was betrothed to Joseph, and, before they became man and wife, it was discovered that she was carrying a child in her womb through the action of the Holy Spirit. Although Joseph,

*her husband, was a man who kept the law, he did not wish
publicly to humiliate her, so he wished to divorce her secretly.
When he was planning this, behold, an angel of the Lord came
to him in a dream. 'Joseph, Son of David,' said the angel, 'do
not hesitate to take Mary as your wife; for that which has
been begotten within her has come from the Holy Spirit. She
will bear a son, and you must call his name Jesus, for it is he
who will save his people from their sins. All this has happened
that there might be fulfilled that which was spoken by the Lord
through the prophet, "Behold, the maiden will conceive and
bear a son, and you must call his name Emmanuel, which
is translated: God with us."' So Joseph woke from his sleep,
and did as the angel of the Lord had commanded him; and he
accepted his wife; and he did not know her until she had borne
a son; and he called his name Jesus.*

To our western ways of thinking, the relationships in this
passage are very bewildering. First, Joseph is said to be
betrothed to Mary; then he is said to be planning quietly to
divorce her; and then she is called his *wife*. But the relationships
represent normal Jewish marriage procedure, in which there
were three steps.

(1) There was the *engagement*. The engagement was
often made when the couple were only children. It was
usually made through the parents, or through a professional
match-maker. And it was often made without the couple
involved ever having seen each other. Marriage was held
to be far too serious a step to be left to the dictates of the
human heart.

(2) There was the *betrothal*. The betrothal was what we
might call the ratification of the engagement into which the

couple had previously entered. At this point the engagement, entered into by the parents or the matchmaker, could be broken if the girl was unwilling to go on with it. But once the betrothal was entered into, it was absolutely binding. It lasted for one year. During that year, the couple were known as husband and wife, although they had not the rights of husband and wife. It could not be terminated in any other way than by divorce. In the Jewish law, we frequently find what is to us a curious phrase. A girl whose fiancé had died during the year of betrothal is called 'a virgin who is a widow'. It was at this stage that Joseph and Mary were. They were betrothed; and if Joseph wished to end the betrothal, he could do so in no other way than by divorce; and in that year of betrothal, Mary was legally known as his wife.

(3) The third stage was *the marriage proper*, which took place at the end of the year of betrothal.

If we remember the normal Jewish wedding customs, then the relationships in this passage are perfectly usual and perfectly clear.

So at this stage it was told to Joseph that Mary was to bear a child, that that child had been begotten by the Holy Spirit, and that he must call the child by the name Jesus. *Jesus* is the Greek form of the Jewish name *Joshua*, and *Joshua* means *Yahweh is salvation*. Long ago, the psalmist had heard God say: 'It is he who will redeem Israel from all its iniquities' (Psalm 130:8). And Joseph was told that the child to be born would grow into the Saviour who would save God's people from their sins. Jesus was not so much the Man born to be King as the Man born to be Saviour. He came to this world, not for his own sake, but for us and for our salvation.

Born of the Holy Spirit

Matthew 1:18–25 (*contd*)

THIS passage tells us how Jesus was born by the action of the Holy Spirit. It tells us of what we call the virgin birth. This is a doctrine which presents us with many difficulties; and we are not compelled to accept it in the literal and the physical sense. This is one of the doctrines on which the Church says that we have full liberty to come to our own conclusion. At the moment, we are concerned only to find out what this means for us.

If we come to this passage with fresh eyes, and read it as if we were reading it for the first time, we will find that what it stresses is not so much that Jesus was born of a woman who was a virgin, as that the birth of Jesus is the work of the Holy Spirit. Mary 'was found to be with child from the Holy Spirit'. 'The child conceived in her is from the Holy Spirit.' It is as if these sentences were underlined, and printed large. That is what Matthew wishes to say to us in this passage. What then does it mean to say that in the birth of Jesus the Holy Spirit of God was specially operative? Let us leave aside all the doubtful and debatable things, and concentrate on that great truth, as Matthew would wish us to do.

In Jewish thought, the Holy Spirit had certain very definite functions. We cannot bring to this passage the *Christian* idea of Holy Spirit in all its fullness, because Joseph would know nothing about that. We must interpret it in the light of the *Jewish* idea of the Holy Spirit, for it is that idea that Joseph would inevitably bring to this message, for that was all he knew.

(1) According to the Jewish idea, *the Holy Spirit was the person who brought God's truth to men and women*. It was the Holy Spirit who taught the prophets what to say; it was the Holy Spirit who taught people of God what to do; it was the Holy Spirit who, throughout the ages and the generations, brought God's truth to men and women. So, Jesus is the one person who brings God's truth to them.

Let us put it in another way. Jesus is the one person who can tell us what God is like and what God means us to be. In him alone, we see what God is and what we ought to be. Before Jesus came, people had only vague and shadowy, and often quite wrong, ideas about God; they could only at best guess and grope; but Jesus could say: 'Whoever has seen me has seen the Father' (John 14:9). In Jesus we see the love, the compassion, the mercy, the seeking heart and the purity of God as nowhere else in all this world. With the coming of Jesus, the time of guessing is gone and the time of certainty is come. Before Jesus came, people did not really know what goodness was. In Jesus alone, we see true humanity, true goodness and true obedience to the will of God. Jesus came to tell us the truth about God and the truth about ourselves.

(2) The Jews believed that the Holy Spirit not only brought God's truth to men and women, but also *enabled them to recognize that truth when they saw it*. So Jesus opens people's eyes to the truth. We are often blinded by our own ignorance; we are led astray by our own prejudices; our minds and eyes are darkened by our own sins and our own passions. Jesus can open our eyes until we are able to see the truth.

In one of William J. Locke's novels, there is a picture of a woman who has any amount of money, and who has spent half a lifetime on a tour of the sights and art galleries of the world. She is weary and bored. Then she meets a Frenchman who has little of this world's goods, but who has a wide knowledge and a great love of beauty. He comes with her, and in his company things are completely different. 'I never knew what things were like,' she said to him, 'until you taught me how to look at them.'

Life is quite different when Jesus teaches us how to look at things. When Jesus comes into our hearts, he opens our eyes to see things truly.

Creation and re-creation

Matthew 1:18–25 (*contd*)

(3) The Jews specially *connected the Spirit of God with the work of creation*. It was through his Spirit that God performed his creating work. In the beginning, the Spirit of God moved upon the face of the waters, and chaos became a world (Genesis 1:2). 'By the word of the Lord the heavens were made,' said the psalmist, 'and all their host by the breath of his mouth' (Psalm 33:6). (Both in Hebrew, *ruach*, and in Greek, *pneuma*, the word for *breath* and *spirit* is the same word.) 'When you send forth your spirit, they are created' (Psalm 104:30). 'The spirit of God has made me,' said Job, 'and the breath of the Almighty gives me life' (Job 33:4).

The Spirit is the Creator of the World and the Giver of Life. So, in Jesus there came into the world God's life-giving and creating power. That power, which reduced the primal chaos to order, came to bring order to our disordered lives. That power, which breathed life where there was no life, has come to breathe life into our weaknesses and frustrations. We could put it this way – we are not really alive until Jesus enters into our lives.

(4) The Jews specially connected the Spirit not only with the work of creation but *with the work of re-creation*. Ezekiel draws his grim picture of the valley of dry bones. He goes on to tell how the dry bones came alive; and then he hears God say: 'I will put my spirit within you, and you shall live' (Ezekiel 37:14). The Rabbis had a saying: 'God said to Israel: "In this world my Spirit has put wisdom in you, but in the future my Spirit will make you to live again."' When people are dead in sin and in lethargy, it is the Spirit of God which can waken them to life anew.

So, in Jesus there came to this world the power which can re-create life. He can bring to life again the soul which is dead in sin; he can revive again the ideals which have died; he can make strong again the will to goodness which has perished. He can renew life when people have lost all that life means.

There is much more in this chapter than the crude fact that Jesus Christ was born of a virgin mother. The essence of Matthew's story is that in the birth of Jesus the Spirit of God was operative as never before in this world. It is the Spirit who brings God's truth to men and women; it is the Spirit who enables them to recognize that truth when they see it; it is the Spirit who was God's agent in the creation of the world; it is the Spirit who alone can re-create the human soul when it has lost the life it ought to have.

Jesus enables us to see what God is and what we ought to be; Jesus opens the eyes of our minds so that we can see the truth of God for us; Jesus is the creating power come among us; Jesus is the re-creating power which can release the souls of men and women from the death of sin.

The birthplace of the king

Matthew 2:1–2

> *When Jesus was born in Bethlehem in Judaea, in the days of Herod the king, behold there came to Jerusalem wise men from the east. 'Where', they said, 'is the newly born King of the Jews? For we have seen his star in its rising and we have come to worship him.'*

IT was in Bethlehem that Jesus was born. Bethlehem was a small town six miles to the south of Jerusalem. In the past, it had been called Ephrath or Ephratah. The name *Bethlehem* means *the House of Bread*, and Bethlehem stood in fertile countryside, which made its name a fitting name. It stood high up on a grey limestone ridge more than 2,500 feet in height. The ridge had a summit at each end, and a hollow like a saddle between them. So, from its position, Bethlehem looked like a town set in an amphitheatre of hills.

Bethlehem had a long history. It was there that Jacob had buried Rachel and had set up a pillar of memory beside her grave (Genesis 48:7, 35:20). It was there that Ruth had lived when she married Boaz (Ruth 1:22), and from Bethlehem Ruth could see the land of Moab, her native land, across the Jordan valley. But above all, Bethlehem was the home and the city of David (1 Samuel 16:1, 17:12, 20:6); and it was for the water of the well of Bethlehem that David longed when he was a hunted fugitive upon the hills (2 Samuel 23:14–15).

In later days, we read that Rehoboam fortified the town of Bethlehem (2 Chronicles 11:6). But in the history of Israel, and to the minds of the people, Bethlehem was uniquely the city of David. It was from the line of David that God was to send the great deliverer of his people. As the prophet Micah had it: 'But you, O Bethlehem of Ephrathah, who are one of the little clans of Judah, from you shall come forth for me one who is to rule in Israel, whose origin is from of old, from ancient days' (Micah 5:2).

It was in Bethlehem, David's city, that the Jews expected great David's greater son to be born; it was there that they expected God's Anointed One to come into the world. And it was so.

The picture of the stable and the manger as the birthplace of Jesus is a picture indelibly etched in our minds; but it may well be that that picture is not altogether correct. Justin Martyr, one of the greatest of the early fathers, who lived about AD 150, and who came from the district near Bethlehem, tells us that Jesus was born in a cave near the village of Bethlehem (Justin Martyr, *Dialogue with Trypho*, 78, 304); and it may well be that Justin's information is correct. The houses in Bethlehem are built on the slope of the limestone ridge; and it is very common for them to have a cave-like stable hollowed out in the limestone rock below the house itself; and very likely it was in such a cave-stable that Jesus was born.

To this day, such a cave is shown in Bethlehem as the birthplace of Jesus, and above it the Church of the Nativity has been built. For a very long time, that cave has been shown as the birthplace of Jesus. It was so in the days of the Roman emperor, Hadrian, who, in a deliberate attempt to desecrate the place, erected a shrine to the heathen god Adonis above it. When the Roman Empire became Christian, early in the fourth century, the first Christian emperor, Constantine, built a great church there, and that church, much altered and often restored, still stands.

The travel writer H. V. Morton tells how he visited the Church of the Nativity in Bethlehem. He came to a great wall, and in the wall there was a door so low that he had to stoop to enter it; and through the door, and on the other side of the wall, there was the church. Beneath the high altar of the church is the cave, and when pilgrims descend into it they find a little cavern about fourteen yards long and four yards wide, lit by silver lamps. In the floor there is a star, and round it a Latin inscription: 'Here Jesus Christ was born of the Virgin Mary.'

When the Lord of Glory came to this earth, he was born in a cave where animals were sheltered. The cave in the Church of the Nativity in Bethlehem may be that same cave, or it may not be. That we will never know for certain. But there is something beautiful in the symbolism that the church where the cave is has a door so low that all must stoop to enter. It is supremely fitting that people should approach the infant Jesus upon their knees.

The homage of the east

Matthew 2:1–2 (contd)

WHEN Jesus was born in Bethlehem, there came to do him homage wise men from the east. The name given to these men is *Magi*, and that is a word which is difficult to translate.

The Greek historian Herodotus (1:101, 132) has certain information about the Magi. He says that they were originally a Median tribe. The Medes were part of the empire of the Persians. They tried to overthrow the Persians and substitute the power of the Medes. The attempt failed. From that time, the Magi ceased to have any ambitions for power or prestige, and became a tribe of priests. They became in Persia almost exactly what the Levites were in Israel. They became the teachers and instructors of the Persian king. In Persia, no sacrifice could be offered unless one of the Magi was present. They became men of holiness and wisdom.

These Magi were men who were skilled in philosophy, medicine and natural science. They were soothsayers and interpreters of dreams. In later times, the word Magus developed a much lower meaning, and came to mean little more than a fortune-teller, a sorcerer, a magician and a charlatan. Such was Elymas, the sorcerer (Acts 13:6, 8), and Simon who is commonly called Simon Magus (Acts 8:9, 11). But at their best the Magi were good and holy men, who sought for truth.

In those ancient days, everyone believed in astrology. People believed that they could foretell the future from the stars, and they believed that a person's destiny was settled by the star under which he or she was born. It is not difficult to see how that belief arose. The stars pursue their unvarying courses; they represent the order of the universe. If then there suddenly appeared some brilliant star, if the unvarying order of the heavens was broken by some special phenomenon, it did look as if God was breaking into his old order and announcing some special thing.

We do not know what brilliant star those ancient Magi saw. Many suggestions have been made. About 11 BC, Halley's comet was visible shooting brilliantly across the skies. About 7 BC, there was a brilliant conjunction of Saturn and Jupiter. In the years 5–2 BC, there was an unusual astronomical phenomenon. In those years, on the first day of the Egyptian month Mesori, Sirius, the dog star, rose heliacally, that is at sunrise, and shone with extraordinary brilliance. Now the name *Mesori* means *the birth of a prince*, and to those ancient astrologers such a star would undoubtedly mean the birth of some great king. We cannot tell what star the Magi saw; but it was their profession to watch the heavens, and some heavenly brilliance spoke to them of the entry of a king into the world.

It may seem to us extraordinary that those men should set out from the east to find a king; but the strange thing is that, just about the time Jesus was born, there was in the world a strange feeling of expectation of the coming of a king. Even the Roman historians knew about this. Not so very much later than this, Suetonius could write: 'There had spread over all the Orient an old and established belief, that it was fated at that time for men coming from Judaea to rule the world' (Suetonius, *Life of Vespasian*, 4:5). Tacitus tells of the same belief that 'there was a firm persuasion ... that at this very time the East was to grow powerful, and rulers coming from Judaea were to acquire universal empire' (Tacitus, *Histories*, 5:13). The Jews had the belief that 'about that time one from their country should become governor of the habitable earth' (Josephus, *The Jewish Wars*, 6:5, 4). At a slightly later time, we find Tiridates, King of Armenia, visiting Nero at Rome with his Magi along with him (Suetonius, *Life of Nero*, 13:1). We find the Magi in Athens sacrificing to the memory of Plato (Seneca, *Epistles*, 58:31). Almost at the same time as Jesus was born, we find Augustus, the Roman emperor, being hailed as the Saviour of the world, and Virgil, the Roman poet, writing his Fourth Eclogue, which is known as the Messianic Eclogue, about the golden days to come.

There is not the slightest need to think that the story of the coming of the Magi to the cradle of Christ is only a lovely legend. It is exactly the kind of thing that could easily have happened in that ancient world. When Jesus Christ came, the world was in an eagerness of expectation. Men and women were waiting for God, and the desire for God was in their hearts. They had discovered that they could not build the golden age without God. It was to a waiting world that Jesus came; and, when he came, the ends of the earth were gathered at his cradle. It was the first sign and symbol of the world conquest of Christ.

The crafty king

Matthew 2:3–9

When Herod the king heard of this he was disturbed, and so was all Jerusalem with him. So he collected all the chief priests and scribes of the people, and asked them where the Anointed One of God was to be born. They said to him, 'In Bethlehem in Judaea. For so it stands written through the prophets, "And you Bethlehem, land of Judah, are by no means the least among the leaders of Judah. For there shall come forth from you the leader, who will be a shepherd to my

*people Israel."' Then Herod secretly summoned the wise men,
and carefully questioned them about the time when the star
appeared. He sent them to Bethlehem. 'Go,' he said, 'and make
every effort to find out about the little child. And, when you
have found him, send news to me, that I too, may come and
worship him.' When they had listened to the king they went
on their way.*

It came to the ears of Herod that the wise men had come
from the east, and that they were searching for the little
child who had been born to be King of the Jews. Any king
would have been worried at the report that a child had been
born who was to occupy his throne. But Herod was doubly
disturbed.

Herod was half-Jew and half-Idumaean. There was
Edomite blood in his veins. He had made himself useful to the
Romans in the wars and civil wars of Palestine, and they
trusted him. He had been appointed governor in 47 BC; in
40 BC he had received the title of king; and he was to reign
until 4 BC. He had wielded power for a long time. He was
called Herod the Great, and in many ways he deserved the
title. He was the only ruler of Palestine who ever succeeded
in keeping the peace and in bringing order to a situation of
disorder. He was a great builder; he was indeed the builder
of the Temple in Jerusalem. He could be generous. In times
of difficulty he cancelled the taxes to make things easier
for the people; and in the famine of 25 BC he had actually
melted down his own gold plate to buy corn for the starving
people.

But Herod had one terrible flaw in his character. He was
almost insanely suspicious. He had always been suspicious,

and the older he became the more suspicious he grew, until, in his old age, he was, as someone said, 'a murderous old man'. If he suspected anyone as a rival to his power, that person was promptly eliminated. He murdered his wife Mariamne and her mother Alexandra. His eldest son, Antipater, and two other sons, Alexander and Aristobulus, were all assassinated by him. Augustus, the Roman emperor, had said, bitterly, that it was safer to be Herod's pig than Herod's son. (The saying is even more epigrammatic in Greek, for in Greek *hus* is the word for a *pig*, and *huios* is the word for a *son*.)

Something of Herod's savage, bitter, warped nature can be seen from the provisions he made when death came near. When he was seventy, he knew that he must die. He retired to Jericho, the loveliest of all his cities. He gave orders that a collection of the most distinguished citizens of Jerusalem should be arrested on trumped-up charges and imprisoned. And he ordered that the moment he died, they should all be killed. He said grimly that he was well aware that no one would mourn for his death, and that he was determined that some tears should be shed when he died.

It is clear how such a man would feel when news reached him that a child was born who was destined to be king. Herod was troubled, and Jerusalem was troubled, too, for Jerusalem knew well the steps that Herod would take to pin down this story and to eliminate this child. Jerusalem knew Herod, and Jerusalem shivered as it waited for his inevitable reaction.

Herod summoned the chief priests and the scribes. The scribes were the experts in Scripture and in the law. The chief priests consisted of two kinds of people. They consisted of ex-high priests. The high priesthood was confined to a very few families. They were the priestly aristocracy, and the members of these select families were called the chief priests. So Herod summoned the religious aristocracy and the theological scholars of his day, and asked them where, according to the Scriptures, the Anointed One of God should be born. They quoted the text in Micah 5:2 to him. Herod sent for the wise men, and despatched them to search diligently for the little child who had been born. He said that he, too, wished to come and worship the child, but his one desire was to murder the child born to be king.

No sooner was Jesus born than we see people grouping themselves into the three groups in which they are always to be found in regard to Jesus Christ. Let us look at the three reactions.

(1) There was the reaction of Herod, *the reaction of hatred and hostility*. Herod was afraid that this little child was going to interfere with his life, his place, his power and his influence, and therefore his first instinct was to destroy him.

There are still those who would gladly destroy Jesus Christ, because they see in him the one who interferes with their lives. They wish to do what they like, and Christ will not let them do what they like; and so they would kill him. People whose one desire is to do what they like never have any use for Jesus Christ. Christians are men and women who have ceased to do what they like, and have dedicated their lives to do as Christ likes.

(2) There was the reaction of the chief priests and scribes, *the reaction of complete indifference*. It did not make the slightest difference to them. They were so engrossed in their Temple ritual and their legal discussions that they completely disregarded Jesus. He meant nothing to them.

There are still those who are so interested in their own affairs that Jesus Christ means nothing to them. The prophet's poignant question can still be asked: 'Is it nothing to you, all you who pass by?' (Lamentations 1:12).

(3) There was the reaction of the wise men, *the reaction of adoring worship*, the desire to lay at the feet of Jesus Christ the noblest gifts which they could bring.

Surely, when we become aware of the love of God in Jesus Christ, we, too, should be lost in wonder, love and praise.

Gifts for Christ

Matthew 2:9–12

And, behold, the star, which they had seen in its rising, led them on until it came and stood over the place where the little child was. When they saw the star, they rejoiced with exceeding great joy. When they came into the house, they saw the little child with Mary, his mother, and they fell down and worshipped him; and they opened their treasures, and offered to him gifts, gold, frankincense and myrrh. And because a message from God came to them in a dream, telling them not to go back to Herod, they returned to their own country by another way.

So the wise men found their way to Bethlehem. We need not think that the star literally moved like a guide across the sky. There is poetry here, and we must not turn lovely poetry into crude and lifeless prose. But over Bethlehem the star was shining. There is a lovely legend which tells how the star, its work of guidance completed, fell into the well at Bethlehem, and that it is still there and can still be seen sometimes by those whose hearts are pure.

Later legends have been busy with the wise men. In the early days, tradition said that there were twelve of them. But now the tradition that there were three is almost universal. The New Testament does not say that there were three, but the idea that there were three no doubt arose from the threefold gift which they brought.

Later legend made them kings. And still later legend gave them names, Caspar, Melchior and Balthasar. Still later legend assigned to each a personal description, and distinguished the gift which each of them gave to Jesus. Melchior was an old man, grey-haired, and with a long beard, and it was he who brought the gift of gold. Caspar was young and beardless, and flushed with youth, and it was he who brought the gift of frankincense. Balthasar was swarthy, with the beard newly grown upon him, and it was he who brought the gift of myrrh.

From very early times, the gifts the wise men brought have been seen as particularly fitting. Each gift has been seen as representing something which specially matched some characteristic of Jesus and his work.

(1) *Gold is the gift of a king*. Seneca, the Roman philosopher, tells us that in Parthia it was the custom that no one could ever approach the king without a gift. And gold, the king of metals, is the fit gift for a king.

So, Jesus was 'the Man born to be King'. But he was to reign not by force but by love; and he was to rule over human hearts, not from a throne, but from a cross.

We do well to remember that Jesus Christ is King. We can never meet Jesus on equal terms. We must always meet him on terms of complete submission. Nelson, the great British admiral, always treated his vanquished opponents with the greatest kindness and courtesy. After one of his naval victories, the defeated admiral was brought aboard Nelson's flagship and on to Nelson's quarterdeck. Knowing Nelson's reputation for courtesy, and thinking to trade upon it, he advanced across the quarterdeck with hand outstretched as if he was advancing to shake hands with an equal. Nelson's hand remained by his side. 'Your sword first,' he said, 'and then your hand.' Before we can be friends with Christ, we must submit to Christ.

(2) *Frankincense is the gift for a priest.* It was in the Temple worship and at the Temple sacrifices that the sweet perfume of frankincense was used. The function of a priest is to open the way to God for men and women. The Latin word for *priest* is *pontifex*, which means a *bridge-builder*. The priest is the one who builds a bridge between human beings and God.

That is what Jesus did. He opened the way to God; he made it possible for us to enter into the very presence of God.

(3) *Myrrh is the gift for one who is to die.* Myrrh was used to embalm the bodies of the dead.

Jesus came into the world to die. Holman Hunt painted a famous picture of Jesus. It shows Jesus at the door of the carpenter's shop in Nazareth. He is still only a young man and has come to the door to stretch his limbs, which have grown cramped over the bench. He stands there in the doorway with arms outstretched, and behind him, on the wall, the setting sun throws his shadow, and it is the shadow of a cross. In the background there kneels Mary, and as she sees that shadow she shields her eyes in fear of coming tragedy.

Jesus came into the world to live for men and women, and, in the end, to die for them. He came to give for us his life and his death.

Gold for a king, frankincense for a priest, myrrh for one who was to die – these were the gifts of the wise men, and, even at the cradle of Christ, they foretold that he was to be the true king, the perfect high priest, and in the end the supreme Saviour of the world.

Escape to Egypt

Matthew 2:13–15

> *When they had gone away, behold, an angel of the Lord appeared in a dream to Joseph. 'Rise,' he said, 'and take the little child and his mother, and flee into Egypt, and stay there until I tell you; for Herod is about to search for the little child, in order to kill him.' So he arose and took the little child and his mother by night and went away into Egypt, and he remained there until the death of Herod. This happened that the word spoken by the Lord through the prophet might be fulfilled: 'Out of Egypt have I called my son.'*

THE ancient world had no doubt that God sent his messages to men and women in dreams. So Joseph was warned in a dream to flee into Egypt to escape Herod's murderous intentions. The flight into Egypt was entirely natural. Often, throughout the troubled centuries before Jesus came, when some peril and some tyranny and some persecution made life intolerable for the Jews, they sought refuge in Egypt. The result was that every city in Egypt had its colony of Jews; and in the city of Alexandria there were actually more than 1,000,000 Jews, and certain districts of the city were entirely handed over to them. Joseph in his hour of peril was doing what many Jews had done before; and when Joseph and Mary reached Egypt they would not find themselves altogether among strangers, for in every town and city they would find Jews who had sought refuge there.

It is an interesting fact that, later on, the enemies of Christianity and the enemies of Jesus used the stay in Egypt as a peg to attach their slanders to him. Egypt was proverbially the land of sorcery, of witchcraft and of magic. The *Talmud* says: 'Ten measures of sorcery descended into the world; Egypt received nine, the rest of the world one.' So the enemies of Jesus declared that it was in Egypt that Jesus had learned a magic and a sorcery which made him able to work miracles and to deceive people.

When the pagan philosopher Celsus directed his attack against Christianity in the third century, an attack that Origen met and defeated, he said that Jesus was brought up as an illegitimate child, that he served for hire in Egypt, that he came to the knowledge of certain miraculous powers, and returned to his own country and used these powers to proclaim himself God (Origen, *Contra Celsum*, 1:38). A certain Rabbi, Eliezer ben Hyrcanus, said that Jesus had the necessary magical formulae tattooed upon his body so that he would not forget them. Such were the slanders that twisted minds connected with the flight to Egypt; but they are obviously false, for it was as a little baby that Jesus was taken to Egypt, and it was as a little child that he was brought back.

Two of the loveliest New Testament legends are connected with the flight into Egypt. The first is about the penitent thief. Legend calls the penitent thief Dismas, and tells that he did not meet Jesus for the first time when they both hung on their crosses on Calvary. The story runs like this. When Joseph and Mary were on their way to Egypt, they were waylaid by robbers. One of the robber chiefs wished to murder them at once and to steal their little store of goods. But something about the baby Jesus went straight to Dismas' heart, for Dismas was one of these robbers. He refused to allow any harm to come to Jesus or his parents. He looked at Jesus and said: 'O most blessed of children, if ever there come a time for having mercy on me, then remember me, and forget not this hour.' So, the legend says, Jesus and Dismas met again at Calvary, and Dismas on the cross found forgiveness and mercy for his soul.

The other legend is a child's story, but it is very lovely. When Joseph and Mary and Jesus were on their way to Egypt, the story runs, as the evening came they were weary, and they sought refuge in a cave. It was very cold, so cold that the ground was white with hoar frost. A spider saw the little baby Jesus, and it wished so much that it could do something to keep him warm in the cold night. It decided to do the only thing it could and spin its web across the entrance of the cave, to make, as it were, a curtain there.

Along the path came a detachment of Herod's soldiers, seeking for children to kill to carry out Herod's bloodthirsty order. When they came to the cave, they were about to burst in to search it, but their captain noticed the spider's web, covered with the white hoar frost and stretched right across the entrance to the cave. 'Look', he said, 'at the spider's web there. It is quite unbroken and there cannot possibly be anyone in the cave, for anyone entering would certainly have torn the web.'

So the soldiers passed on, and left the holy family in peace, because a little spider had spun its web across the entrance to the cave. And that, so they say, is why to this day we put tinsel on our Christmas trees, for the glittering tinsel streamers stand for the spider's web, white with the hoar frost, stretched across the entrance of the cave on the way to Egypt. It is a lovely story; and this much, at least, is true, that no gift which Jesus receives is ever forgotten.

The last words of this passage introduce us to a custom which is characteristic of Matthew. He sees in the flight to Egypt a fulfilment of the word spoken by Hosea. He quotes it in the form: 'Out of Egypt I have called my son.' That is a quotation from Hosea 11:1, which reads: 'When Israel was a child, I loved him, and out of Egypt I called my son.'

It can be seen at once that in its original form this saying of Hosea had nothing to do with Jesus, and nothing to do with the flight to Egypt. It was nothing more than a simple statement of how God had delivered the nation of Israel from slavery and from bondage in the land of Egypt.

We shall see, again and again, that this is typical of Matthew's use of the Old Testament. He is prepared to use as a prophecy about Jesus any text at all which can be made verbally to fit, even though originally it had nothing to do with the question in hand, and was never meant to have anything to do with it. Matthew knew that almost the only way to convince the Jews that Jesus was the promised Anointed One of God was to prove that he was the fulfilment of Old Testament prophecy. And in his eagerness to do that, he finds prophecies in the Old Testament where no prophecies were ever meant. When we read a passage like this, we must remember that, though it seems strange and unconvincing to us, it would appeal to those Jews for whom Matthew was writing.

The slaughter of the children

Matthew 2:16–18

> *Then Herod saw that he had been tricked by the wise men, and he sent and slew all the children in Bethlehem, and in all the districts near by. He slew every child of two years and under, reckoning from the time when he had made his inquiries from the wise men. Then the word which was spoken through Jeremiah the prophet was fulfilled: 'A voice was heard in Rama, weeping and much lamenting, Rachel weeping for her children, and she refused to be comforted, for they were no more.'*

WE have already seen that Herod was a past master in the art of assassination. He had no sooner come to the throne than he began by annihilating the Sanhedrin, the supreme court of the Jews. Later he slaughtered 300 court officers out of hand. Later still he murdered his wife Mariamne, and her mother Alexandra, his eldest son Antipater, and two other sons, Alexander and Aristobulus. And in the hour of his death he arranged for the slaughter of the notable men of Jerusalem.

It was not to be expected that Herod would calmly accept the news that a child had been born who was going to be king. We have read how he had carefully inquired of the wise men when they had seen the star. Even then, he was craftily working out the age of the child so that he might take steps towards murder; and now he put his plans into swift and savage action. He gave orders that every child under two years of age in Bethlehem and the surrounding district should be slaughtered.

There are two things which we must note. First, Bethlehem was not a large town, and the number of the children would not be greater than twenty to thirty babies. We must not think in terms of hundreds. It is true that this does not make Herod's crime any the less terrible, but we must get the picture right.

Second, there are certain critics who hold that this slaughter cannot have taken place because there is no mention of it in any writer outside this one passage of the New Testament. The Jewish historian Josephus, for instance, does not mention it. There are two things to be said. First, as we have just seen, Bethlehem was a comparatively small place, and in a land where murder was so widespread the slaughter of twenty or thirty babies would cause little stir, and would mean very little except to the broken-hearted mothers of Bethlehem. Second, the nineteenth-century historian Thomas Macaulay, in his famous *History of England*, points out that John Evelyn, the well-known seventeenth-century diarist, who was a most assiduous and voluminous recorder of contemporary events, never mentions the massacre of Glencoe. The fact that a thing is not mentioned, even in the places where one might expect it to be mentioned, is no proof at all that it did not happen. The whole incident is so typical of Herod that we need not doubt that Matthew is passing the truth down to us.

Here is a terrible illustration of what some people will do to get rid of Jesus Christ. If they are set on their own course, if they see in Christ someone who is liable to interfere with their ambitions and rebuke their ways, their one desire is to eliminate Christ; and then they are driven to the most terrible things, for if they do not break others physically, they will break their hearts.

Again, at the end of this passage, we see Matthew's characteristic way of using the Old Testament. He quotes Jeremiah 31:15, 'Thus says the Lord: A voice is heard in Ramah, lamentation and bitter weeping. Rachel is weeping for her children; she refuses to be comforted for her children, because they are no more.'

The verse in Jeremiah has no connection with Herod's slaughter of the children. The picture in Jeremiah was this. Jeremiah was picturing the people of Jerusalem being led away in exile. On their sad way to an alien land, they pass Ramah, and Ramah was the place where Rachel lay buried (1 Samuel 10:2); and Jeremiah pictures Rachel weeping, even in the tomb, for the fate that had befallen the people.

Matthew is doing what he so often did. In his eagerness, he is finding a prophecy where no prophecy is. But, again, we must remind ourselves that what seems strange to us seemed in no way strange to those for whom Matthew was writing in his day.

Return to Nazareth

Matthew 2:19–23

> *When Herod died, behold, the angel of the Lord appeared in a dream to Joseph in Egypt. 'Rise,' he said, 'and take the little child and his mother, and go into the land of Israel. For those who seek the little child's life are dead.' So he rose and took the little child and his mother, and went into the land of Israel. When he heard that Archelaus was king in Judaea instead of Herod, his father, he was afraid to go there. So, when he had received a message from God in a dream, he withdrew to the districts of Galilee, and he came and settled in a town called Nazareth. This happened so that the word spoken through the prophets might be fulfilled: 'He shall be called a Nazarene.'*

In due time Herod died, after which the whole kingdom over which he had ruled was split up. The Romans had trusted Herod, and they had allowed him to reign over a very considerable territory; but Herod knew perfectly well that none of his sons would be allowed the same degree of power. So he had divided his kingdom into three, and in his will he had left a part to each of three of his sons. He had left Judaea to Archelaus, Galilee to Herod Antipas, and the region away to the north-east and beyond Jordan to Philip.

But the death of Herod did not solve the problem. Archelaus was a bad king, and he was not to last long upon the throne. In fact, he had begun his reign with an attempt to out-Herod Herod, for he had opened his rule with the deliberate slaughter of 3,000 of the most influential people in the country. Clearly, even now that Herod was dead, it was still unsafe to return to Judaea with the savage and reckless Archelaus on the throne. So Joseph was guided to go to Galilee, where Herod Antipas, a much better king, reigned.

It was in Nazareth that Joseph settled, and it was in Nazareth that Jesus was brought up. It must not be thought that Nazareth was a quiet little backwater, quite out of touch with life and with events.

Nazareth lay in a hollow in the hills in the south of Galilee. But a young boy had only to climb the hills for half the world to be at his door. He could look west and the waters of the Mediterranean, blue in the distance, would meet his eyes; and he would see the ships going out to the ends of the earth. He had only to look at the plain which skirted the coast, and he would see, slipping round the foot of the very hill on which he stood, the road from Damascus to Egypt, the land bridge to Africa. It was one of the greatest caravan routes in the world.

It was the road by which, centuries before, Joseph had been sold down into Egypt as a slave. It was the road that, 300 years before, Alexander the Great and his legions had followed. It was the road by which, centuries later, Napoleon was to march. It was the road which, in the twentieth century, General Sir Edmund Allenby was to take. Sometimes it was called the Way of the South, and sometimes the Road of the Sea. On it, Jesus would see all kinds of travellers from all kinds of nations on all kinds of errands, coming and going from the ends of the earth.

But there was another road. There was the road which left the sea coast at Acre or Ptolemais and went out to the east. It was the Road of the East. It went out to the eastern bounds and frontiers of the Roman Empire. Once again, the cavalcade of the caravans and their silks and spices would be continually on it; and on it also the Roman legions clanked out to the frontiers.

Nazareth indeed was no backwater. Jesus was brought up in a town where the ends of the earth passed the foot of the hilltop. From his boyhood days, he was confronted with scenes which must have spoken to him of a world for God.

We have seen how Matthew clinches each event in the early life of Jesus with a passage from the Old Testament which he regards as a prophecy. Here, Matthew cites a prophecy: 'He shall be called a Nazarene'; and here Matthew has set us an insoluble problem, for there is no such text in the Old Testament. In fact, Nazareth is never mentioned in the Old Testament. No one has ever satisfactorily solved the problem of what part of the Old Testament Matthew has in mind.

The ancient writers liked puns and plays on words. It has been suggested that Matthew is playing on the words of Isaiah in Isaiah 11:1: 'A shoot shall come out from the stock of Jesse, and a branch shall grow out of his roots.' The word for *branch* is *nezer*; and it is just possible that Matthew is playing on the word *Nazarene* and the word *nezer*; and that he is saying at one and the same time that Jesus was from *Nazareth* and that Jesus was the *nezer*, the promised branch from the stock of Jesse, the descendant of David, the promised anointed king of God. No one can tell. What prophecy Matthew had in mind must remain a mystery.

So now the stage is set: Matthew has brought Jesus to Nazareth, and in a very real sense Nazareth was the gateway to the world.

Introduction to Luke

A historian's care

First and foremost, Luke's gospel is an exceedingly careful bit of work. His Greek is notably good. The first four verses are well-nigh the best Greek in the New Testament. In them he claims that his work is the product of the most careful research. His opportunities were ample and his sources must have been good. As the trusted companion of Paul he must have known all the great figures of the Church, and we may be sure that he had them tell their stories to him. For two years he was Paul's companion in imprisonment in Caesarea. In those long days he had every opportunity for study and research and he must have used them well.

An example of Luke's care is the way in which he dates the emergence of John the Baptist. He does so by no fewer than six contemporary datings. 'In the fifteenth year of the reign of Tiberius Caesar [1], Pontius Pilate being governor of Judaea [2], Herod being tetrarch of Galilee [3], and his brother Philip being tetrarch of the region of Ituraea and Trachonitis [4], and Lysanias tetrarch of Abilene [5] in the high priesthood of Annas and Caiaphas [6], the word of God came to John' (Luke 3:1–2, Revised Standard Version). Here is a man who is writing with care and who will be as accurate as it is possible for him to be.

The gospel for the Gentiles

It is clear that Luke wrote mainly for Gentiles. The book was written to a man called Theophilus, a high official in the Roman government. Theophilus was a Gentile, as was Luke himself, and there is nothing in the gospel that a Gentile could not grasp and understand. (1) As we have seen, Luke begins his dating from the reigning *Roman* emperor and the current *Roman* governor. The *Roman* date comes first. (2) Unlike Matthew, he is not greatly interested in the life of Jesus as the fulfilment of Jewish prophecy. (3) He very seldom quotes the Old Testament at all. (4) He has a habit of giving Hebrew words in their Greek equivalent so that a Greek would understand. Simon the *Cananaean* becomes Simon the *Zealot* (cf. Luke 6:15; Matthew 10:4). *Calvary* is called not by its Hebrew name, *Golgotha*, but by its Greek name, *Kranion*. Both mean *the place of a skull*. He never uses the Jewish term *Rabbi* of Jesus but always a Greek word meaning *Master*. When he is tracing the descent of Jesus, he traces it not to Abraham, the founder of the Jewish race, as Matthew does, but to Adam, the founder of the human race (cf. Matthew 1:2; Luke 3:38).

Because of this Luke is the easiest of all the gospels to read.

The gospel of women

In Palestine the place of women was low. In the Jewish morning prayer a man thanked God that he has not made him 'a Gentile, a slave or a woman'. But Luke gives a very special place to women. The birth narrative is told from Mary's point of view. It is in Luke that we read of Elizabeth, of Anna, of the widow at Nain, of the woman who anointed Jesus' feet in the house of Simon the Pharisee. It is Luke who makes vivid the pictures of Martha and Mary and of Mary Magdalene. It is very likely that Luke was a native of Macedonia where women held a more emancipated position than anywhere else; and that may have something to do with it.

The gospel of praise

In Luke the phrase *praising God* occurs oftener than in all the rest of the New Testament put together. This praise reaches its peak in the three great hymns that the Church has sung throughout all her generations – the *Magnificat* (1:46–55), the *Benedictus* (1:68–79) and the *Nunc Dimittis* (2:29–32). There is a radiance in Luke's gospel which is a lovely thing, as if the sheen of heaven had touched the things of earth.

The universal gospel

But the outstanding characteristic of Luke is that it is the universal gospel. All the barriers are down; Jesus Christ is for all people without distinction.

(a) The kingdom of heaven is not shut to the Samaritans (9:51–6). Luke alone tells the parable of the Good Samaritan (10:30–7). The one grateful leper is a Samaritan (17:11–19). John can record a saying that the Jews have no dealings with the Samaritans (John 4:9). But Luke refuses to shut the door on anyone.

(b) Luke shows Jesus speaking with approval of Gentiles whom an orthodox Jew would have considered unclean. He shows us Jesus citing the widow of Zarephath and Naaman the Syrian as shining examples (4:25–7). The Roman centurion is praised for the greatness of his faith (7:9). Luke tells us of that great word of Jesus, 'People will come from east and west, from north and south, and will eat in the kingdom of God' (13:29).

(c) Luke is supremely interested in the poor. When Mary brings the offering for her purification it is the offering of the poor (2:24). When Jesus is, as it were, setting out his credentials to the emissaries of John, the climax is, 'The poor have good news brought to them' (7:22). He alone tells the parable of the rich man and the poor man (16:19–31). In Luke's account of the beatitudes the saying of Jesus runs, not, as in Matthew (5:3), 'Blessed are the poor in spirit', but simply, 'Blessed are you who are poor' (Luke 6:20). Luke's gospel has been called 'the gospel of the underdog'. His heart runs out to everyone for whom life is an unequal struggle.

(d) Above all Luke shows Jesus as the friend of outcasts and sinners. He alone tells of the woman who anointed Jesus' feet and bathed them with her tears and wiped them with her hair in the house of Simon the Pharisee (7:36–50); of Zachaeus, the despised tax-gatherer (19:1–10); of the penitent thief (23:43); and he alone has the immortal story of the prodigal son and the loving father (15:11–32). When Matthew tells how Jesus sent his disciples out to preach, he says that Jesus told them not to go to the Samaritans or the Gentiles (Matthew 10:5); but Luke omits that altogether. All four gospel writers quote from Isaiah 40 when they give the message of John the Baptist, 'Prepare the way of the Lord; make straight in the desert a highway for our God'; but only Luke continues the quotation to its triumphant conclusion, 'And all flesh shall see the salvation of God' (Isaiah 40:3–5; Matthew 3:3; Mark 1:3; John 1:23; Luke 3:4, 6). Luke of all the gospel writers sees no limits to the love of God.

Luke

A historian's introduction

Luke 1:1–4

Since many have set their hands to the task of drawing up an account of the events which were completed among us, telling the story just as those who were the original eyewitnesses and who became the servants of the word handed it down to us, I too made up my mind to carry out a careful investigation of all things from the beginning, and to write to you, Theophilus, your excellency, an orderly account of them, so that you might have in your mind a full and reliable account of the things in which you have been instructed.

LUKE's introduction is unique in the first three gospels because it is the only place where the author steps out upon the stage and uses the pronoun 'I'. There are three things to note in this passage.

(1) It is the best bit of Greek in the New Testament. Luke uses here the very form of introduction which the great Greek historians all used. Herodotus begins, 'These are the researches of Herodotus of Halicarnassus.' A much later historian, Dionysius of Halicarnassus, tells us at the

beginning of his history, 'Before beginning to write I gathered information, partly from the lips of the most learned men with whom I came into contact, and partly from histories written by Romans of whom they spoke with praise.' So Luke, as he began his story in the most sonorous Greek, followed the highest models he could find.

It is as if Luke said to himself, 'I am writing the greatest story in the world and nothing but the best is good enough for it.' Some of the ancient manuscripts are very beautiful productions, written in silver ink on purple vellum; and often the scribe, when he came to the name of God or of Jesus, wrote it in gold. The story is told of an old workman who, every Friday night, took the newest and shiniest coins out of his pay packet for Sunday's offering in church. The historian, the scribe and the workman were all filled with the same idea – only the best is good enough for Jesus. They always gave their utmost for the highest.

(2) It is most significant that Luke was not satisfied with anyone else's story of Christ. He must have his own. Real religion is never a second-hand thing. It is a personal discovery. Professor Arthur Gossip of Trinity College, Glasgow, used to say that the four gospels were important, but beyond them all came the gospel of personal experience. Luke had to rediscover Jesus Christ for himself.

(3) There is no passage of the Bible which sheds such a floodlight on the doctrine of the inspiration of Scripture. No one would deny that the gospel of Luke is an inspired document; and yet Luke begins by affirming that it is the product of the most careful historical research. God's inspiration does not come to those who sit with folded hands and lazy minds and only wait, but to those who think and

seek and search. True inspiration comes when the searching mind joins with the revealing Spirit of God. The word of God is given, but it is given to those who search for it. 'Search and you will find' (Matthew 7:7).

A son is promised

Luke 1:5–25

In the time of Herod, the king of Judaea, there was a priest called Zacharias, who belonged to the section of Abia. His wife was also a direct descendant of Aaron and her name was Elizabeth. Both of them were good people before God, for they walked blamelessly in all the commandments and ordinances of the Lord. They had no child because Elizabeth was barren and both of them were far advanced in years. When he was acting as priest before God, when his section was on duty, in accordance with the custom of priestly duty, it fell to him by lot to go into the Temple of the Lord to burn the incense. The whole congregation of the people was praying outside at the hour when incense was offered. The angel of the Lord appeared to him, standing at the right side of the altar of incense. When Zacharias saw him he was deeply moved and awe fell upon him. The angel said to him, 'Do not be afraid, Zacharias, because your request has been heard and your wife Elizabeth will bear you a son and you must call him by the name of John. You will have joy and exultation and many will rejoice at his birth. He will be great in God's sight; he must not drink wine or strong drink and, even from the time he is in his mother's womb, he will be filled with the Holy Spirit. He will turn many sons of Israel to the Lord their God; and he himself will go before his face in the spirit and the power of Elijah, to turn the hearts of the fathers to the children, and the disobedient to the wisdom of the just, to get ready a people prepared for the Lord.' Zacharias said to the angel, 'How will I know that this is going to happen? For I am an old man and my wife is far advanced in years.' 'I am Gabriel,' the angel answered, 'who stands before God, and I have been sent to speak to you and to tell you this good news. And — look you — you will be silent and unable to speak until the day these things happen, because you did not believe my words which will be fulfilled in their own time.' The people were waiting for Zacharias and they were surprised that he was lingering so long in the Temple. When he came out he was not able to speak to them and they realized that he had seen a vision in the Temple. He kept making signs to them but he remained unable to speak. When the days of his time of service were completed he went away to his own home. After these days Elizabeth his wife conceived; and she hid herself for five months. 'This is God's doing for me,' she said, 'when he looked upon me to take away my shame among men.'

Zacharias, the central character in this scene, was a priest. He belonged to the section of Abia. Every direct descendant of Aaron was automatically a priest. That meant that for all ordinary purposes there were far too many priests. They were therefore divided into twenty-four sections. Only at the Passover, at Pentecost and at the Feast of Tabernacles did all the priests serve. For the rest of the year each course served two periods of one week each. Priests who loved their work looked forward to that week of service above all things; it was the highlight of their lives.

A priest might marry only a woman of absolutely pure Jewish lineage. It was specially meritorious to marry a woman who was also a descendant of Aaron, as was Elizabeth, the wife of Zacharias.

There were as many as 20,000 priests altogether and so there were not far short of 1,000 in each section. Within the sections all the duties were allocated by lot. Every morning and evening sacrifice was made for the whole nation. A burnt offering of a male lamb, one year old, without spot or blemish was offered, together with a meat offering of flour and oil and a drink offering of wine. Before the morning sacrifice and after the evening sacrifice incense was burned on the altar of incense so that, as it were, the sacrifices might go up to God wrapped in an envelope of sweet-smelling incense. It was quite possible that many a priest would never have the privilege of burning incense all his life; but if the lot did fall on any priest, that day was the greatest day in all his life, the day he longed for and dreamed of. On this day the lot fell on Zacharias and he would be thrilled to the core of his being.

But in Zacharias' life there was tragedy. He and Elizabeth were childless. The Jewish Rabbis said that seven people were excommunicated from God and the list began, 'A Jew who has no wife, or a Jew who has a wife and who has no child.' Childlessness was a valid ground for divorce. Not unnaturally Zacharias, even on his great day, was thinking of his personal and domestic tragedy and was praying about it. Then the wondrous vision came and the glad message that, even when hope was dead, a son would be born to him.

The incense was burned and the offering made in the inmost court of the Temple, the Court of the Priests. While the sacrifice was being made, the congregation thronged the next court, the Court of the Israelites. It was the privilege of the priest at the evening sacrifice to come to the rail between the two courts after the incense had been burned in order to bless the people. The people marvelled that Zacharias was so long delayed. When he came he could not speak and the people knew that he had seen a vision. So in a wordless daze of joy Zacharias finished his week's duty and went home; and then the message of God came true and Elizabeth knew she was going to have a child.

One thing stands out here. *It was in God's house that God's message came to Zacharias.* We may often wish that a message from God would come to us. In George Bernard Shaw's play, *Saint Joan*, Joan hears voices from God. The Dauphin is annoyed. 'Oh, your voices, your voices,' he said, 'Why don't the voices come to me? I am king not you.' 'They do come to you,' said Joan, 'but you do not hear them. You have not sat in the field in the evening listening for them. When the angelus rings you cross yourself and have done with it; but if you prayed from your heart, and listened to the thrilling of the bells in the air after they stop ringing, you would hear the voices as well as I do.' Joan gave herself the chance to hear God's voice. Zacharias was in the Temple waiting on God. God's voice comes to those who listen for it – as Zacharias did – in God's house.

God's message to Mary

Luke 1:26–38

> *In the sixth month the angel Gabriel was sent from God to a town of Galilee called Nazareth, to a maiden who was betrothed to a man called Joseph, who belonged to the house of David. The maiden's name was Mary. He came in to her and said, 'Greetings, most favoured one. The Lord is with you.' She was deeply moved at this word and wondered what a greeting like that could mean. The angel said to her, 'Do not be afraid, Mary, for you have found favour in God's sight. Look you – you will conceive and you will bear a son and you must call him by the name of Jesus. He will be great and he will be called the Son of the Most High; and the Lord God will give him the throne of David his father; and he will rule over the house of Jacob forever, and there will be no end to his kingdom.' Mary said to the angel, 'How can this be since I do not know a man?' The angel answered, 'The Holy Spirit will come upon you and the Spirit of the Most High will overshadow you, and so the child who will be born will be called holy, the Son of God, and – look you – Elizabeth, too, your kinswoman has also conceived in her old age; and this is now the sixth month for her who is called barren, because there is nothing which is impossible with God.' Mary said, 'I am the Lord's servant. Whatever he says, I accept.' And the angel went away from her.*

MARY was betrothed to Joseph. Betrothal lasted for a year and was quite as binding as marriage. It could be dissolved only by divorce. Should the man to whom a girl was betrothed die, in the eyes of the law she was a widow. In the law there occurs the strange-sounding phrase, 'a virgin who is a widow'.

In this passage we are face to face with one of the great controversial doctrines of the Christian faith – the virgin birth. The Church does not insist that we believe in this doctrine. Let us look at the reasons for and against believing in it, and then we may make our own decision.

There are two great reasons for accepting it.

(1) The literal meaning of this passage, and still more of Matthew 1:18–25, clearly is that Jesus was to be born of Mary without a human father.

(2) It is natural to argue that if Jesus was, as we believe, a very special person, he would have a special entry into the world.

Now let us look at the things which may make us wonder if the story of the virgin birth is to be taken as literally as all that.

(1) The genealogies of Jesus both in Luke and in Matthew (Luke 3:23–38; Matthew 1:1–17) trace the genealogy of Jesus through *Joseph*, which is strange if Joseph was not his real father.

(2) When Mary was looking for Jesus on the occasion that he lingered behind in the Temple, she said, 'Your father and I have been searching for you in great anxiety' (Luke 2:48). The name *father* is definitely given by Mary to Joseph.

(3) Repeatedly Jesus is referred to as Joseph's son (Matthew 13:55; John 6:42).

(4) The rest of the New Testament knows nothing of the virgin birth. True, in Galatians 4:4 Paul speaks of Jesus as 'born of woman'. But this is the natural phrase for any human being (cf. Job 14:1, 15:14, 25:4).

But let us ask, 'If we do not take the story of the virgin birth literally, how did it arise?' The Jews had a saying that in the birth of *every* child there are three partners – the father, the mother and the Spirit of God. They believed that no child could ever be born without the Spirit. And it may well be that the New Testament stories of the birth of Jesus are lovely, poetical ways of saying that, even if he had a human father, the Holy Spirit of God was operative in his birth in a unique way.

In this matter we may make our own decision. It may be that we will desire to cling to the literal doctrine of the virgin birth; it may be that we will prefer to think of it as a beautiful way of stressing the presence of the Spirit of God in family life.

Mary's submission is a very lovely thing. 'Whatever God says, I accept.' Mary had learned to forget the world's commonest prayer – 'Your will be *changed*' – and to pray the world's greatest prayer – 'Your will be *done*.'

The paradox of blessedness

Luke 1:39–45

In those days Mary arose and went eagerly to the hill country, to a city of Judah, and went into the house of Zacharias and greeted Elizabeth. When Elizabeth heard Mary's greeting the babe leaped in her womb and Elizabeth was filled with the Holy Spirit, and she lifted up her voice with a great cry and said, 'Blessed are you among women and blessed is the fruit of your womb. Why has this been granted to me – that the mother of

> *my Lord should come to me? For – look you – when the voice of*
> *your greeting came to my ears the babe in my womb leaped with*
> *exultation. Blessed is she who believed that the things spoken to*
> *her from the Lord would find their fulfilment.'*

THIS is a kind of lyrical song on the blessedness of Mary. Nowhere can we better see the paradox of blessedness than in her life. To Mary was granted the blessedness of being the mother of the Son of God. Well might her heart be filled with a wondering, tremulous joy at so great a privilege. Yet that very blessedness was to be a sword to pierce her heart. It meant that some day she would see her son hanging on a cross.

To be chosen by God so often means at one and the same time a crown of joy and cross of sorrow. The piercing truth is that God does not choose a person for ease and comfort and selfish joy but for a task that will take all that head and heart and hand can bring to it. *God chooses us in order to use us.* When Joan of Arc knew that her time was short she prayed, 'I shall only last a year; use me as you can.' When that is realized, the sorrows and hardships that serving God may bring are not matters for lamentation; they are our glory, for all is suffered for God.

When Richard Cameron, the Covenanter, was caught by the dragoons they killed him. He had very beautiful hands and they cut them off and sent them to his father with a message asking if he recognized them. 'They are my son's,' he said, 'my own dear son's. Good is the will of the Lord who can never wrong me or mine.' The shadows of life were lit by the sense that they, too, were in the plan of God. A great Spanish saint prayed for his people, 'May God deny you peace and give you glory.' One great preacher said, 'Jesus Christ came not to make life easy but to make men great.'

It is the paradox of blessedness that it confers on a person at one and the same time the greatest joy and the greatest task in all the world.

A wondrous hymn

Luke 1:46–56

> And Mary said, 'My soul magnifies the Lord, and my spirit has exulted in God, my Saviour, because he looked graciously on the humble estate of his servant. For – look you – from now on all generations shall call me blessed, for the Mighty One has done great things for me and his name is holy. His mercy is from generation to generation to those who fear him. He demonstrates his power with his arm. He scatters the proud in the plans of their hearts. He casts down the mighty from their seats of power. He exalts the humble. He fills those who are hungry with good things and he sends away empty those who are rich. He has helped Israel, his son, in that he has remembered his mercy – as he said to our fathers that he would – to Abraham and to his descendants forever.'

HERE we have a passage which has become one of the great hymns of the Church – the *Magnificat*. It is steeped in the Old Testament; and is closely related to Hannah's song of praise in 1 Samuel 2:1–10. It has been said that religion is the opiate of the people; but it has also been said that the *Magnificat* is the most revolutionary document in the world.

It speaks of three of the revolutions of God.

(1) *He scatters the proud in the plans of their hearts.* That is a *moral* revolution. Christianity is the death of pride. Why? Because if people set their lives beside that of Christ, it tears away the last vestiges of their pride.

Sometimes something happens to us which with a vivid, revealing light shames us. The American writer O. Henry has a short story about a boy who was brought up in a village. In school he used to sit beside a girl and they were fond of each other. He went to the city and fell into evil ways. He became a pickpocket and a petty thief. One day he snatched an old lady's purse. It was clever work and he was pleased. And then he saw coming down the street the girl whom he used to know, still sweet with the radiance of innocence. Suddenly he saw himself for the cheap, vile thing he was. Burning with shame, he leaned his head against the cool iron of a lamp standard. 'God,' he said, 'I wish I could die.' He saw himself.

Christ enables us to see ourselves. It is the death-blow to pride. The moral revolution has begun.

(2) *He casts down the mighty – he exalts the humble.* That is a *social* revolution. Christianity puts an end to the world's labels and prestige.

Muretus was a wandering scholar of the middle ages. He was poor. In an Italian town he became ill and was taken to a hospital for waifs and strays. The doctors were discussing his case in Latin, never dreaming he could understand. They suggested that since he was such a worthless wanderer they might use him for medical experiments. He looked up and answered them in their own learned tongue, 'Call no man worthless for whom Christ died.'

When we have realized what Christ did for each and every one of us, it is no longer possible to regard anyone as being beneath us. The social grades are gone.

(3) *He has filled those who are hungry – those who are rich he has sent empty away.* That is an *economic* revolution. A non-Christian society is an acquisitive society where people are out for as much as they can get. A Christian society is a society where no one dares to have too much while others have too little, where everyone must get only to give away.

There is loveliness in the *Magnificat* but in that loveliness there is dynamite. Christianity brings about a revolution in individuals and revolution in the world.

His name is John

Luke 1:57–66

When Elizabeth's time to bear the child was completed she brought forth a son. When her neighbours and kinsfolk heard that the Lord had shown great mercy to her they rejoiced with her. On the eighth day they went to circumcise the child and it was their intention to call him Zacharias after his father. But his mother said, 'No; he must be called John.' They said to her, 'There is no one in your connection who is called by this name.' They asked his father by signs by what name he wished him to be called. He asked for a writing tablet and wrote, 'John is his name.' Immediately his mouth was opened and his tongue was loosed and he kept on praising God. And great awe fell upon all the neighbours, and all

> *these events were talked about in all the hill country of Judaea;*
> *and all those who heard them kept them in their hearts and*
> *said, 'What will this child turn out to be, for the hand of the*
> *Lord is with him?'*

In Palestine the birth of a boy was an occasion of great joy. When the time of the birth was near at hand, friends and local musicians gathered near the house. When the birth was announced and it was a boy, the musicians broke into music and song, and there was universal congratulation and rejoicing. If it was a girl the musicians went silently and regretfully away! There was a saying, 'The birth of a male child causes universal joy, but the birth of a female child causes universal sorrow.' So in Elizabeth's house there was double joy. At last she had a child and that child was a son.

On the eighth day the boy was circumcised and received his name. Girls could be named any time within thirty days of their birth. In Palestine names were descriptive. They sometimes described a circumstance attending the birth as *Esau* and *Jacob* do (Genesis 25:25–6). They sometimes described the child. *Laban*, for instance, means *white* or *blonde*. Sometimes the child received the parental name. Often the name described the parents' joy. *Saul* and *Samuel*, for instance, both mean *asked for*. Sometimes the name was a declaration of the parents' faith. *Elijah*, for instance, means *Yahweh is my God*. Thus in a time of Baal worship Elijah's parents asserted their faith in the true God.

Elizabeth, to the neighbours' surprise, said that her son must be called John and Zacharias indicated that that was also his desire. *John* is a shorter form of the name

Jehohanan, which means *Yahweh's gift* or *God is gracious*. It was the name which God had ordered to be given to the child and it described the parents' gratitude for an unexpected joy.

It was the question of the neighbours and of all who had heard the amazing story, 'What will this child turn out to be?' Every child is a bundle of possibilities. There was an old Latin teacher who always bowed gravely to his class before he taught them. When he was asked why, he answered, 'Because you never know what one of these pupils will turn out to be.' The entry of a child into a family is two things. First, it is the greatest privilege which life can offer a husband and wife. It is something for which to thank God. Second, it is one of life's supreme responsibilities, for that child is a bundle of possibilities, and on parents and teachers depends how these possibilities will or will not be realized.

A father's joy

Luke 1:67–80

His father Zacharias was filled with the Holy Spirit and prophesied like this: 'Blessed be the Lord, the God of Israel, because he has graciously visited his people and wrought deliverance for them. He has raised the horn of salvation for us in the house of David, his servant – as long ago he said he would through the mouth of his holy prophets – even deliverance from our enemies and from the hand of all who hate us, in that he has shown mercy to us as he did to our fathers and has remembered his holy covenant, the pledge which he gave

*to Abraham our father, to grant to us that we, being delivered
from the hands of our enemies, should fearlessly serve him, in
holiness and righteousness before him, all our days. And you,
child, shall be called the prophet of the Most High; for you will
walk before the Lord to prepare his ways, in order to give the
knowledge of salvation to his people together with forgiveness
of their sins, through the mercy of our God, in which the dawn
from on high has graciously visited us, to shine upon those who
sit in darkness and in the shadow of death, and to direct our
feet in the way of peace.'*

*And the child grew and was strengthened by the Spirit; and
he lived in the desert places until the day when he was displayed
to Israel.*

ZACHARIAS had a great vision for his son. He thought of him as
the prophet and the forerunner who would prepare the way
of the Lord. All devout Jews hoped and longed for the day
when the Messiah, God's anointed king, would come. Most
of them believed that, before he came, a forerunner would
announce his coming and prepare his way. The usual belief
was that Elijah would return to do so (Malachi 4:5). Zacharias
saw in his son the one who would prepare the way for the
coming of God's king.

Verses 75–7 give a great picture of the steps of the
Christian way.

(1) There is *preparation*. All life is a preparation to lead
us to Christ. When Sir Walter Scott was young his aim was
to be a soldier. An accident made him slightly lame and that
dream had to be abandoned. He took to reading the old
Scottish histories and romances and so became the master
novelist. An old man said of him, 'He was makin' himsell

a' the time; but he didna ken maybe what he was about till years had passed.' In life God is working all things together to bring us to Christ.

(2) There is *knowledge*. It is the simple fact that there was no real understanding of what God was like until Jesus came. The Greeks thought of a passionless God, beyond all joy and sorrow, looking on humanity in calm unmoved detachment – no help there. Jews thought of a demanding God, whose name was law and whose function was that of judge – nothing but fear there. Jesus came to tell that God was love, and in staggered amazement people said, 'We never knew that God was like that.' One of the great functions of the incarnation was to bring to men and women the knowledge of God.

(3) There is *forgiveness*. We must be clear about one thing regarding forgiveness. It is not so much the remission of penalty as the restoration of a relationship. Nothing can deliver us from certain consequences of our sins; the clock cannot be put back; but estrangement from God is turned to friendship, the distant God has become near and the God we feared has become the lover of human souls.

(4) There is *walking* in the ways of peace. *Peace* in Hebrew does not mean merely freedom from trouble; it means all that makes for our highest good; and through Christ we are enabled to walk in the ways that lead to everything that means life, and no longer to all that means death.

Journey to Bethlehem

Luke 2:1–7

In these days a decree went out from Caesar Augustus that a census should be taken of all the world. The census first took place when Quirinius was governor of Syria; and everyone went to enrol himself, each man to his own town. So Joseph went up from Galilee, from the town of Nazareth, to Judaea, to David's town, which is called Bethlehem, because he belonged to the house and the line of David, to enrol himself with Mary who was betrothed to him and she was with child. When they arrived there her time to bear the child was completed; and she bore her first-born son and wrapped him in swaddling clothes and laid him in a manger because there was no room for them in the place where they had meant to lodge.

In the Roman Empire periodical censuses were taken with the double object of assessing taxation and of discovering those who were liable for compulsory military service. The Jews were exempt from military service, and, therefore, in Palestine a census would be predominantly for taxation purposes. Regarding these censuses, we have definite information as to what happened in Egypt; and almost certainly what happened in Egypt happened in Syria, too, and Judaea was part of the province of Syria. The information we have comes from actual census documents written on papyrus and then discovered in the dust-heaps of Egyptian towns and villages and in the sands of the desert.

Such censuses were taken every fourteen years. And from AD 20 until about AD 270 we possess actual documents from every census taken. If the fourteen-year cycle held good in Syria this census must have been in 8 BC and that was the year in which Jesus was born. It may be that Luke has made one slight mistake. Quirinius did not actually become governor of Syria until AD 6; but he held an official post previously in those regions from 10 BC until 7 BC and it was during that first period that this census must have been taken.

Critics used to question the fact that every man had to go to his own city to be enrolled; but here is an actual government edict from Egypt:

> Gaius Vibius Maximus, Prefect of Egypt orders: 'Seeing that the time has come for the house-to-house census, it is necessary to compel all those who for any cause whatsoever are residing outside their districts to return to their own homes, that they may both carry out the regular order of the census, and may also diligently attend to the cultivation of their allotments.'

If that was the case in Egypt, it may well be that in Judaea, where the old tribal ancestries still held good, men had to go to the headquarters of their tribe. Here is an instance where further knowledge has shown the accuracy of the New Testament.

The journey from Nazareth to Bethlehem was eighty miles. The accommodation for travellers was most primitive. The eastern khan was like a series of stalls opening off a common courtyard. Travellers brought their own food; all that the innkeeper provided was fodder for the animals and a fire to cook. The town was crowded and there was no room for Joseph and Mary. So it was in the common courtyard that

Mary's child was born. Swaddling clothes consisted of a square of cloth with a long bandage-like strip coming diagonally off from one corner. The child was first wrapped in the square of cloth and then the long strip was wound round and round about him. The word translated *manger* means a place where animals feed; and therefore it can be either the stable or the manger which is meant.

That there was no room in the inn was symbolic of what was to happen to Jesus. The only place where there was room for him was on a cross. He sought an entry to the overcrowded hearts of those around him; he could not find it; and still his search – and his rejection – go on.

Shepherds and angels

Luke 2:8–20

> *In this country there were shepherds who were in the fields, keeping watch over their flock by night. An angel of the Lord appeared to them and the glory of the Lord shone round about them and they were much afraid. The angel said to them, 'Do not be afraid; for – look you – I am bringing you good news of great joy, which will be to every people, for today a Saviour has been born for you, in David's town, who is Christ the Lord. You will recognize him by this sign. You will find the babe wrapped in swaddling clothes and laid in a manger.' And suddenly with the angel there was a crowd of heaven's host, praising God and saying, 'In the highest heights glory to God; and on earth peace to the men whose welfare he ever seeks.' When the angels had left them and gone away to heaven, the shepherds said to each other, 'Come! Let us go across to*

Bethlehem and let us see this thing which has happened which
the Lord has made known to us.' So they hurried on and they
discovered Mary and Joseph, and the babe lying in a manger.
When they had seen him they told everyone about the word
which had been spoken to them about this child; and all who
heard were amazed at what was told them by the shepherds.
But Mary stored up these things in her memory and in her
heart kept wondering what they meant. So the shepherds
returned glorifying and praising God for all that they had
seen, just as it had been told to them.

It is a wonderful thing that the story should tell that the first
announcement of God came to some shepherds. Shepherds
were despised by the orthodox good people of the day.
They were quite unable to keep the details of the ceremonial
law; they could not observe all the meticulous handwashings
and rules and regulations. Their flocks made constant
demands on them; and so the orthodox looked down on
them. It was to simple men of the fields that God's message
first came.

But these were in all likelihood very special shepherds. We
have already seen how in the Temple, morning and evening,
an unblemished lamb was offered as a sacrifice to God. To see
that the supply of perfect offerings was always available the
Temple authorities had their own private sheep flocks; and
we know that these flocks were pastured near Bethlehem. It is
most likely that these shepherds were in charge of the flocks
from which the Temple offerings were chosen. It is a lovely
thought that the shepherds who looked after the Temple
lambs were the first to see the Lamb of God who takes away
the sin of the world.

We have already seen that when a boy was born, the local musicians congregated at the house to greet him with simple music. Jesus was born in a stable in Bethlehem and therefore that ceremony could not be carried out. It is lovely to think that the minstrelsy of heaven took the place of the minstrelsy of earth, and angels sang the songs for Jesus that the earthly singers could not sing.

All through these readings we must have been thinking of the rough simplicity of the birth of the Son of God. We might have expected that, if he had to be born into this world at all, it would be in a palace or a mansion. There was a European monarch who worried his court by often disappearing and walking incognito among his people. When he was asked not to do so for security's sake, he answered, 'I cannot rule my people unless I know how they live.' It is the great thought of the Christian faith that we have a God who knows the life we live because he too lived it and claimed no special advantage over ordinary people.